ARMORED ANIMALS

BY HERBERT S. ZIM

ILLUSTRATED BY RENÉ MARTIN

William Morrow and Company   New York

71- 101794

The author wishes to thank Dr. Hobart M. Smith
of the University of Colorado, Boulder, Colorado,
for checking the manuscript.

A Rogewinn Book

Printed in the United States of America.

Library of Congress Catalog Card Number 78-133243

1   2   3   4   5   75   74   73   72   71

The animal world is full of beauty, but it is also tough and dangerous—a world of eat or be eaten. It is a world in which every wild animal has had to find a place for itself and its young in order to survive.

Among the many kinds of animals are a number of unusual ones with built-in armor. Thousands of animals that live on land or in the water have some kind of hard, tough, or spiny covering to protect them. They seem to be well equipped for survival.

In one sense, all animals are armored animals. Each has some kind of skin or cover to protect its living tissues from the outside world. Even single-celled microscopic animals are surrounded by a membrane. Jellyfish, caterpillars, frogs, or lizards are all, to some degree, protected from elements of their surroundings that might hurt them.

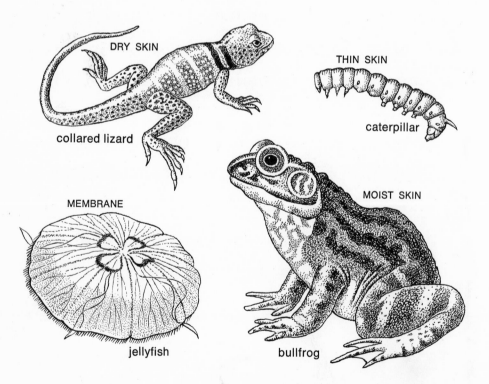

DRY SKIN

collared lizard

THIN SKIN

caterpillar

MEMBRANE

MOIST SKIN

jellyfish

bullfrog

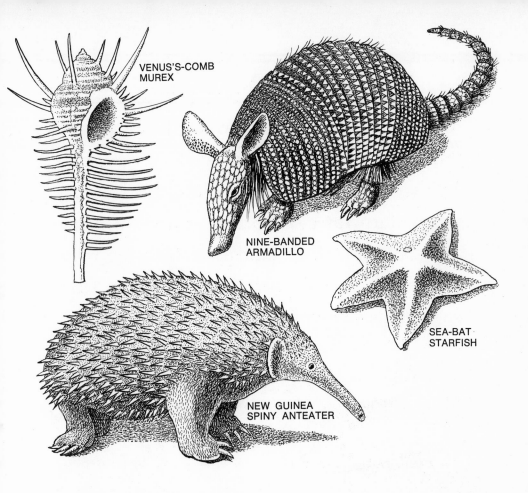

VENUS'S-COMB
MUREX

NINE-BANDED
ARMADILLO

SEA-BAT
STARFISH

NEW GUINEA
SPINY ANTEATER

But truly armored animals are further protected against being eaten. They may be covered by shell or bone, by heavy scales or plates, or by hairs that have been altered into sharp quills.

All animals live by eating plants or other animals. In fact, they may be divided into three great feeding groups. First are the herbivores—animals that feed on plants. Next are the carnivores—animals that feed on flesh, that is, on other animals. Third are the omnivores—animals like ourselves that feed on both plants and animals.

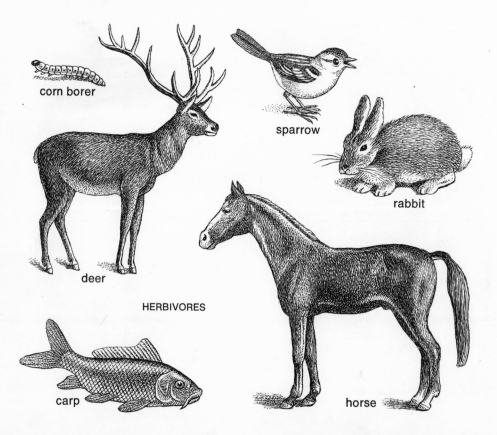

corn borer

sparrow

rabbit

deer

HERBIVORES

carp

horse

flycatcher

frog

CARNIVORES

anteater

lion

snake

OMNIVORES

bear

robin

pig

boy

Animals that are the food supply for the meat eaters have developed a number of ways to keep from being eaten. The antelope is swift and may escape the lion chasing after it. Its speed is good protection. Other animals can hide easily, because they are small or because their coloring camouflages them. Some are so well concealed that they cannot be seen even a few feet away.

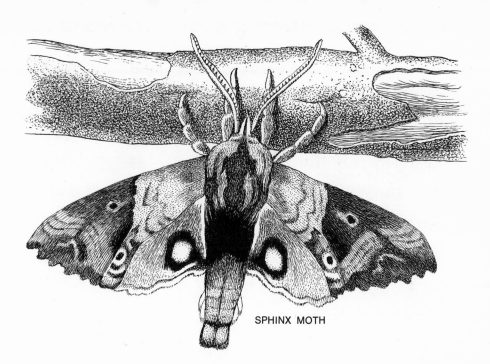

SPHINX MOTH

Still other animals are marked so they confuse the hunter. One lizard has a stumpy tail that looks like its head. As a result, an enemy does not know which end to attack. Certain butterflies and moths, when they open their wings quickly, display a large eyespot that may scare a predator.

Chemical protection works well, too. The animal that is hunted may have a bad odor, like a skunk, or a bad taste, like a monarch butterfly. Or the animal may secrete a poisonous substance that will injure the attacker. Some toads form a poison in their skin, which may kill dogs that bite them.

THE MONARCH,
a milkweed butterfly,
is avoided by birds perhaps
because of its bad taste.

THE VICEROY,
an admiral butterfly,
unrelated to the monarch,
looks like it and may be
protected for this reason.

If a hunted animal does not have these protections, it may imitate an animal that does. This imitation is called mimicry. A viceroy butterfly, which may taste good, mimics the monarch butterfly, which is believed to be bad tasting. Birds that feed on butterflies avoid both the monarchs and the viceroys.

Then certain animals are protected by warning behavior. A hunted animal may spring from concealment with a flash of color on its body, wings, or tail. It will spread its wings to their fullest or assume a bold, menacing posture that will scare off the hunter.

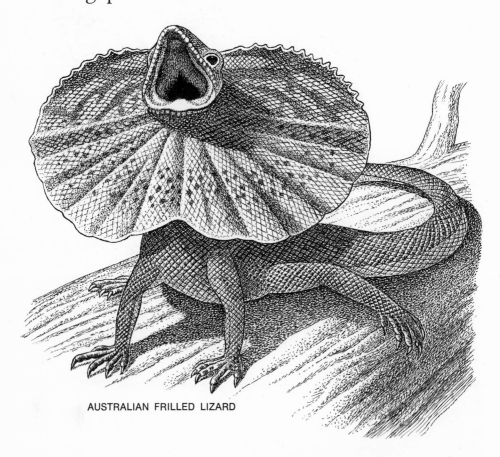

AUSTRALIAN FRILLED LIZARD

But of the many ways animals protect themselves, the most impressive is armor. This form of defense is widespread. Armor takes the form of shells, plates, pads, scales, spikes, and spines. It can be very effective.

All the world's animals are classified into a dozen or so large groups called phyla. Armored animals are found in about half of these phyla. The total number of animals with some sort of armor is considerable.

Most animals are invertebrates, or without a backbone. Many invertebrates have armor or at least some kind of outside skeleton. Often this covering is hard and heavy, almost like a rock. Sometimes it is thin and light, but tough. In any case, all the armor of invertebrates is lifeless material. The armor of backboned animals is quite different.

NUMMULITES
(enlarged)

Even a few of the smallest and simplest animals—those that are only a single living cell—have armor. Two groups of protozoa have hard coverings. As billions upon billions of these animals live and die, their shells pile up and form thick layers of rock. From one such kind of rock, made of nummulites (disk-like shells), people long ago built the great pyramids of Egypt.

The most famous of the armored invertebrates are the mollusks, or shellfish, a large
group of about 50,000 species. Most mollusks
grow a shell in which the animal lives. This
varied, multicolored armor is familiar to all
and the delight of shell collectors. One group
of shellfish lives in single-coiled, spiral shells,
with a cover that shuts the opening when
the animal is safe inside. These gastropod
animals include the conchs, the whelks, cone
shells, and their many kin.

Another group of mollusks lives between
two shells that open on a hinge, so the animal can get food and water, and can even
move about. But the shells can shut tightly
together when the animal is in danger. These
hinged shellfish include the clams, mussels,
scallops, and oysters.

SEA SNAILS

alphabet cone shell

operculum (lid)

turban shell

pear whelk

California horn shell

moon shell

limpet

tulip shell

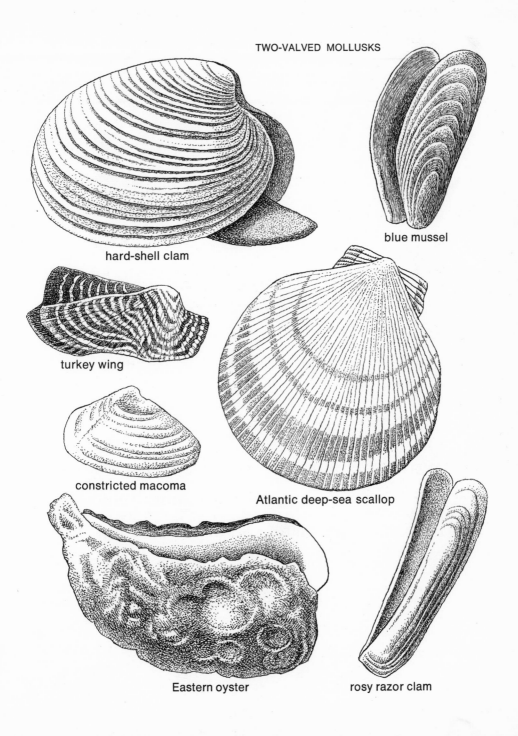

TWO-VALVED MOLLUSKS

hard-shell clam

blue mussel

turkey wing

constricted macoma

Atlantic deep-sea scallop

Eastern oyster

rosy razor clam

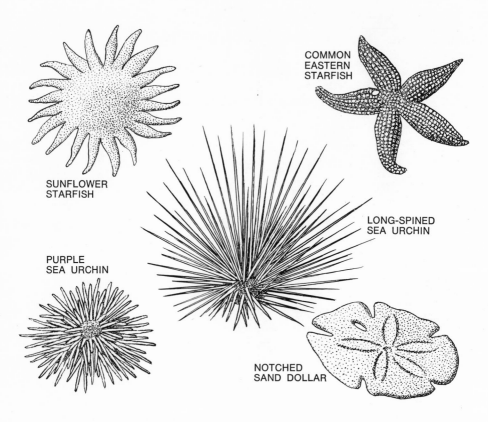

SUNFLOWER
STARFISH

COMMON
EASTERN
STARFISH

LONG-SPINED
SEA URCHIN

PURPLE
SEA URCHIN

NOTCHED
SAND DOLLAR

Starfish and their relatives are also armored. The starfish is covered with short spines and armored limy plates. Some sea urchins have heavier armor, and one kind has spines over six inches long, edged with sawlike teeth.

Still another group of armored water animals are the crustaceans, of which there are some 25,000 kinds. They include shrimps, lobsters, and crabs, together with many hundreds of smaller species. Each of these animals has an outer skeleton made somewhat like your fingernail—thin, tough, and horny. It has joints for movement, and some have spikes and spines. The animal's muscles are attached to this outside skeleton. With these muscles it moves its legs and tail, swims, and hunts for food. Thus the outer skeleton provides for both movement and protection.

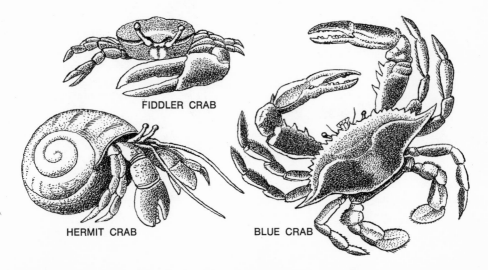

FIDDLER CRAB

HERMIT CRAB

BLUE CRAB

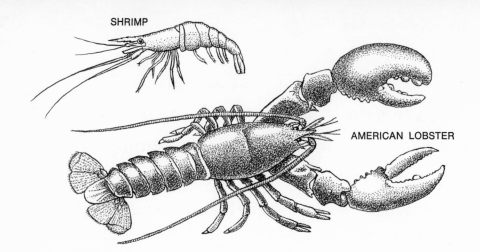

SHRIMP

AMERICAN LOBSTER

Barnacles are unusual crustaceans. The tiny young swim freely. Soon they settle down, grow heavy plates of lime, and become anchored and armored for life.

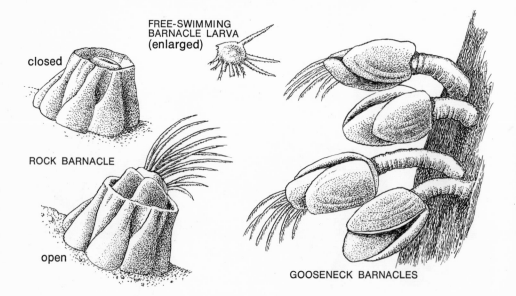

closed

FREE-SWIMMING
BARNACLE LARVA
(enlarged)

ROCK BARNACLE

open

GOOSENECK BARNACLES

THE HORSESHOE CRAB, whose ancestors lived nearly 500 million years ago, is one of the oldest of the armored animals alive today.

Insects—the largest group of invertebrates—also have a horny type of outer skeleton, though among many of them it is quite soft. But one order, the beetles, is very well armored. Head and legs are enclosed in a hard sheath, as is much of the body. The first pair of rigid wings protects the beetle's back. The second, thinner pair, is used in flight.

DIVING BEETLE

BURYING BEETLE

CATERPILLAR HUNTER

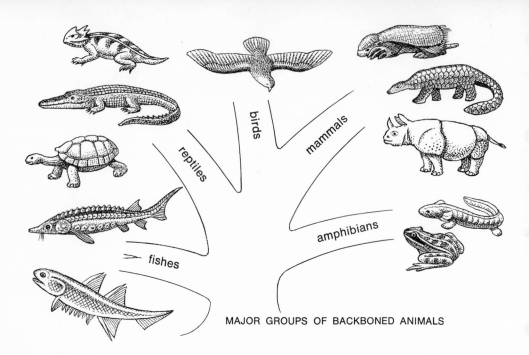

MAJOR GROUPS OF BACKBONED ANIMALS

At the top of the animal kingdom is the great group of vertebrates, the backboned animals. A number of them are armored, too. Vertebrates fall into five large groups, or classes: the fishes, amphibians (frogs, toads, and salamanders), reptiles (snakes, lizards, turtles), birds, and mammals. All of these classes, except for the birds, include animals with some kind of armor.

Animals without backbones have muscles attached to their outer skeleton. Animals with backbones have muscles attached to their inner skeleton of bone. This way of supporting muscles helps backboned animals to grow larger and move fast. Speed helps vertebrates and is the way many get food and escape being eaten. When backboned animals have armor, it is clearly an extra kind of protection and not necessary for movement.

So, the armor of vertebrates has formed as part of the outer skin. Scales, plates, or spikes usually are made by bone cells that deposit hard chemical salts in the skin. This kind of armor is living tissue, not the dead secretion that invertebrates form. Most of the armor of larger backboned animals is made of bone.

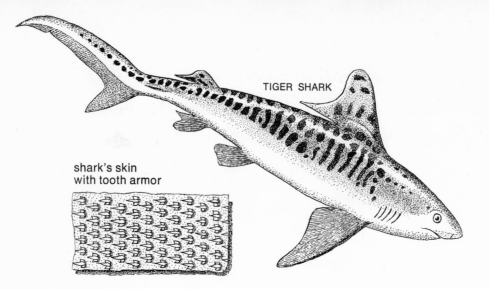

TIGER SHARK

shark's skin
with tooth armor

The armor of backboned animals has developed in three ways. Among the early fishes, and also among sharks, the cells that make the hard inside of teeth also grow in the fish's skin, where they form thousands of small, toothlike bumps. These bumps are so hard and plentiful that the fish's skin becomes armor. While living sharks hardly can be called armored animals, their skin, full of tiny hard "teeth," is unusually tough.

The second, and more common, kind of armor develops from cells that make bone. This armor plate is true bone—a substance quite different from the dentine of teeth. Bone is not as hard as tooth material, and it grows more rapidly.

The third armor material is keratin, the stuff that makes hair, nails, horn, and scales.

Some of the first fishes that lived half a billion years ago were armored. They were small, slow moving, and lacked the kind of jaws that fishes have today. Fossils show that plates of armor covered their heads. Some had armor on the sides and back also.

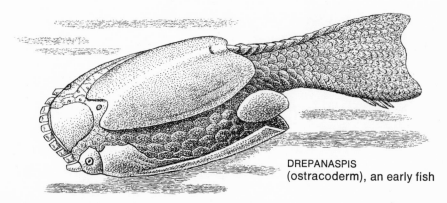

DREPANASPIS
(ostracoderm), an early fish

A number of living fishes are armored, too. Of several dozen kinds, best known are the gars and sturgeons. The tough, diamond-shaped scales of gars and the larger plates of sturgeons are alike. Sturgeons grow ten to twelve feet long. Their small, dark eggs are the expensive delicacy called caviar.

Today sturgeons are quite rare. Rivers where some live have become polluted. Since armor is no protection against chemicals and waste, experts predict that these sturgeons cannot long survive.

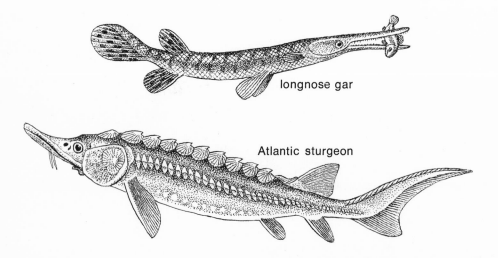

longnose gar

Atlantic sturgeon

Other kinds of armored fishes live in the ocean, mainly in shallow water. The trunk-fish, as firmly boxed as a trunk, is one example. Only its small fins and tail can move. The puffer, when in danger, actually blows itself up into a spiny, armored ball. The file-

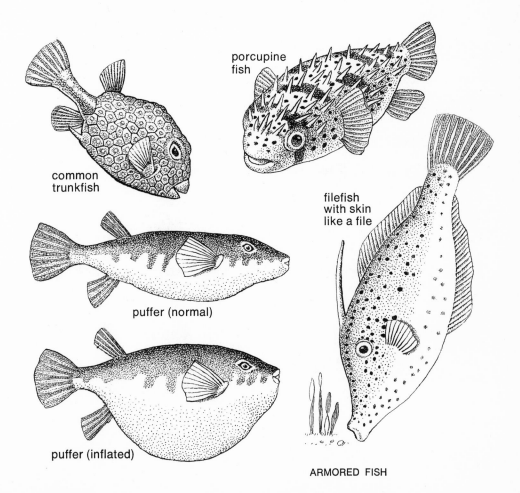

porcupine fish

common trunkfish

filefish with skin like a file

puffer (normal)

puffer (inflated)

ARMORED FISH

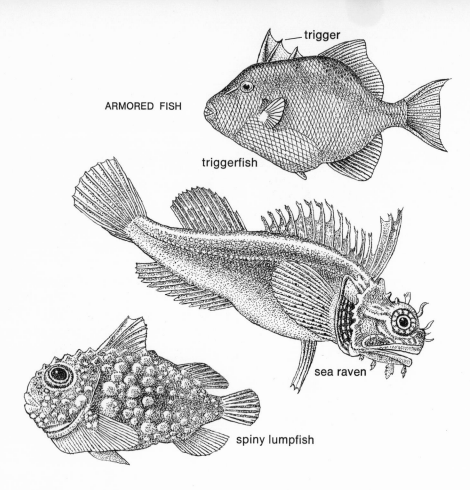

trigger

ARMORED FISH

triggerfish

sea raven

spiny lumpfish

fish and the triggerfish also have armored skins. The large, bony spine on the back of the triggerfish locks into place when it is raised and comes down only when the trigger —a shorter spine behind it—is pulled.

Less armored and somewhat of a mystery is the sea horse, a kind of semiarmored fish. It is covered with thin, horny plates instead of scales. Most sea horses are only a few inches long and are not at all like usual fish. The armored tail is not used for swimming, but can be looped for grasping and holding onto seaweed. The fins are small, and the head tapers into a long, armored snout.

PIPEFISH

SEA HORSE

Neither the sea horse nor its relative the pipefish seems well able to protect itself or even to survive. Yet both do. They hide in shallow beds of sea grass where they have few enemies. Perhaps this behavior is better protection than armor.

Although no living amphibian has armor, a few show a trace of it. Also, ancient amphibians were armored. Fossils of some show dermal plates embedded in the skin. Some ancient amphibians also had large, heavy skulls, which were an extra protection.

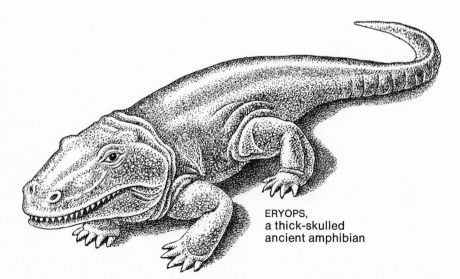

ERYOPS,
a thick-skulled
ancient amphibian

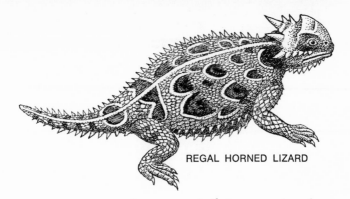
REGAL HORNED LIZARD

In contrast to the amphibians, nearly every group of reptiles has developed some kind of armor at some time or another. Of the modern reptiles, snakes are the only large group that lacks armor. Their skin is made of overlapping, horny scutes. The scutes on small snakes are fine, offering little protection. However, they help the snake move along in tight places.

Lizards have scutes very much like those of snakes. A few have a bit of bony armor, too. The horned lizards, for example, have a crest of spines across the head and smaller spines along the back, sides, and tail.

Best known of all armored animals are the common, everyday turtles. Here are reptiles so well protected they have survived for some 200 million years. Most of the 200 kinds of turtles alive today are flourishing.

The skin of turtles, like that of snakes, has horny scutes that cover the exposed parts of the body. In addition, patches of bone form over the upper ribs and on the underside as overgrown, wider ribs. These bones join together forming an upper shell (carapace) and a lower shell (plastron) tied together by bridges of bone.

WOOD TURTLE

PAINTED TURTLE

SPOTTED TURTLE

BOX TURTLE
(closed)

BOX TURTLE

GALÁPAGOS TORTOISE

Between these two bony shells are the turtle's organs and muscles. Most turtles can pull their head, long neck, and legs between the shells for protection. The box turtles have a hinged bottom shell and can close it for the most complete protection of all.

Some turtles live for a century or more and grow to great size, like the land tortoises of the Galápagos and Mauritius Islands. Fossil bones of a giant tortoise, Archelon, from India, show it may have been twelve feet long with a three-foot skull.

The largest turtles today are sea animals. One of them, the leatherback, grows six to eight feet long and may weigh up to fifteen hundred pounds. But for all their built-in protection, the large turtles (like the green) have been reduced in number and are threatened with extinction. Whalers once stowed hundreds of the now rare Galápagos tortoises aboard ship as a supply of fresh meat.

Turtles have lived on earth a hundred times as long as man. Apparently their armor has served them well. But turtles have not progressed to become a dominant animal group. Moreover, their armor offers little protection against man and his weapons.

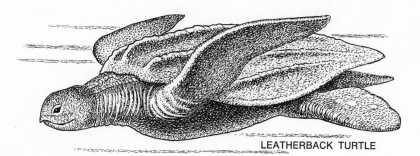

LEATHERBACK TURTLE

CROCODILES
have many bony plates in
their skin, as well as extra ribs.
7 pairs of
abdominal ribs

Alligators, crocodiles, and caimans look a bit like overgrown lizards. However, they are an older, more primitive, and better armored group. Most cannot move around very well on land. All have protective bony plates and pads of tough, fibrous tissues in their skin. Riblike bars protect and support their weak underside.

Alligators and crocodiles are carnivores that feed on fish, birds, and even on mammals that come to the water's edge to drink. They have no real enemies except man. During the past century alligators and crocodiles, hunted for their skin, have become less and less common.

ALLIGATOR

CROCODILE

CAIMAN

Distant relatives of crocodiles were among
the first reptiles. They lived long before any
dinosaurs were known. One group included
Placodus, a slow, ten-foot creature that fed
on shellfish. Fossil remains show it had thick
protective ribs; others had a heavily armored
back. They were the first armored reptiles.

PLACODUS,
a placodont

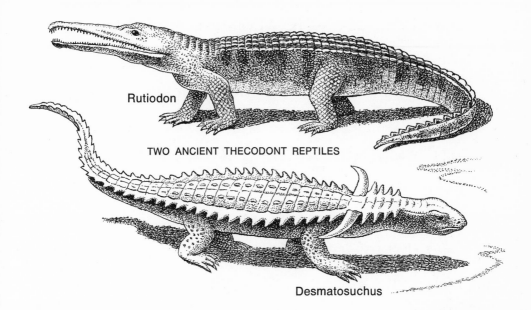

Rutiodon

TWO ANCIENT THECODONT REPTILES

Desmatosuchus

Thecodont reptiles (some 200 million years ago) included a number that looked more like crocodiles, though still only distantly related. Rutiodon was twelve feet long; some of its relatives were much larger. Another group, of which Desmatosuchus is an example, had a double row of armor down their backs.

Armor is for defense, so carnivores should have little need of it. Alligators, crocodiles, and all their ancestors seem an exception. These animals spend much of their time quietly waiting in the water or dozing in the sun. Without armor they might fall prey to faster or more cunning predators. Perhaps this way of life explains why they have armor.

Aided by armor, or in spite of it, crocodiles and their close kin have been around for some 150 million years. One early crocodile with a six-foot head grew nearly fifty feet long.

Of all the armored reptiles, the best known are several of the now extinct dinosaurs. One of the first and most unusual was Stegosaurus, which had a double row of bony plates down its back and four spines on its tail. Its sides had no protection at all.

STEGOSAURUS

SCELIDOSAURUS

ANKYLOSAURUS

Not much later came Ankylosaurus and its relatives, low, flattened, heavily armored beasts with spikes, spines, and bony nodules over their back. All dinosaurs of the Ankylosaurus group displayed this type of armor. Nodosaurus had spines on its head and even larger bony plates and spines on its back. Its tail was a bony club.

These living armored forts squatted down when attacked, their legs tucked beneath the body, thus exposing nothing to the enemy but bony plates and spines. In this position a clubbing tail could still be used—and it was.

In Ceratops, still another herbivore group, horned and armored dinosaurs gradually developed from unarmored ancestors. These dinosaurs had massive head armor, often with one or more spearlike spikes. A circle of Ceratops in defense formation might indeed defeat larger attackers. Even the charge of a single one could rout a predator.

Fossils show a variety of these armored dinosaurs. Some had a single horn on the nose; some had three horns on the skull; some had five. Most developed a heavy fringed skull. A few had additional armor on their back and sides. Although most Ceratops dinosaurs were armored, they could also move around reasonably well in search of plant food.

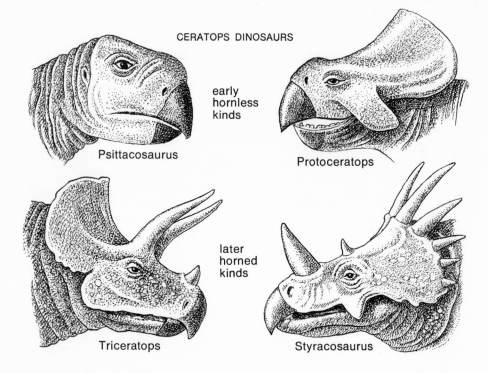

CERATOPS DINOSAURS

early
hornless
kinds

Psittacosaurus

Protoceratops

later
horned
kinds

Triceratops

Styracosaurus

The Mesozoic era, or Age of Reptiles, lasted for some 170 million years. The horned dinosaurs appeared toward the close of that period, which ended about 65 million years ago. By that time the dinosaurs and all the other great reptiles had died off. Not a single dinosaur remained.

TYRANNOSAURUS

TRICERATOPS

For a long time dinosaurs were a large and successful group. Why they became extinct when conditions changed is not clear. But obviously armor made no difference. The armored dinosaurs died off with the others. Whatever protection armor gives, it is not protection against change.

In contrast to the reptiles, only a few mammals are armored. True enough, some large mammals, like the elephant and hippopotamus, have tough, heavy hides, but they are not armored.

Of five species of rhinoceros, two have hard scales and tubercules embedded in their skin. If the huge rhinoceros is considered as truly armored, it is the largest armored animal alive today.

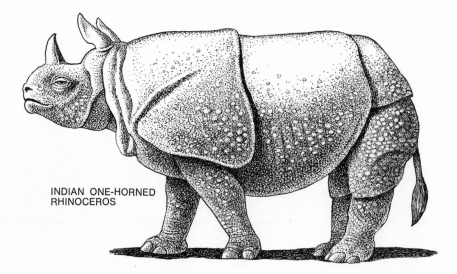

INDIAN ONE-HORNED
RHINOCEROS

Other present-day armored mammals are smaller than the rhinoceros. They include some covered with spines like hedgehogs and porcupines, some enclosed in armored plates like armadillos, and some covered with sharp scales like pangolins.

Among the mammals with spiny armor are the odd and rare echidnas, wrongly called spiny anteaters. Only one other mammal, the platypus, lays eggs as the echidnas do. All other mammals have young that develop inside the mother's body till birth.

SHORT-NOSED ECHIDNA

rolled in a ball for protection

Five kinds of echidnas live in or near Australia. They differ only slightly in their spiny protection. Yellowish spines, two to three inches long, cover their back completely. The spines are hollow, sharp, and lack bristles. Some reports say they are poisonous.

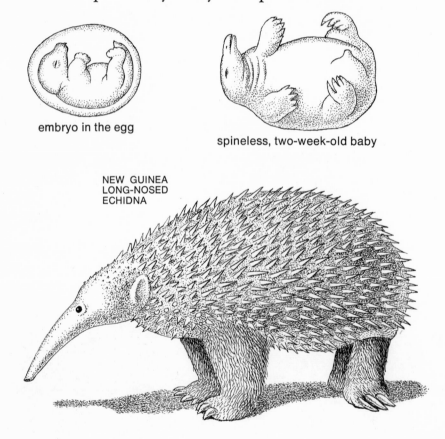

embryo in the egg

spineless, two-week-old baby

NEW GUINEA
LONG-NOSED
ECHIDNA

HEDGEHOG

rolled up

SMALL
MADAGASCAR
HEDGEHOG

Somewhat better protected are the hedgehogs. This group includes six species of small
animals found in Europe, Africa, and Asia.
Their spines are short and sharp. When a
hedgehog rolls into a spiny ball, it is safe
indeed. Hedgehogs feed on insects and other
small land animals.

Probably the best protected of the spiny mammals are porcupines, rodents that are relatives of mice and squirrels. Porcupine spines are long and barbed at the tip. When they stick into the face of a dog or a fox, the barbs hold tightly and do not come out easily. No wonder most predators learn to beware of porcupines.

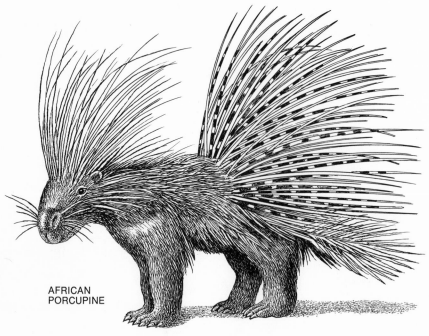

AFRICAN
PORCUPINE

Old World porcupines live
on the open ground and in burrows.

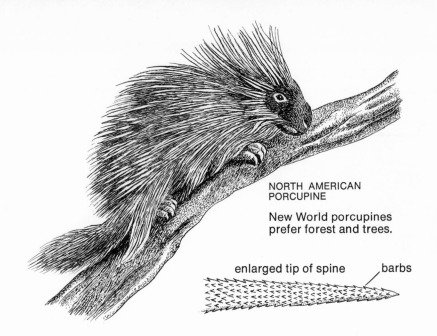

NORTH AMERICAN
PORCUPINE

New World porcupines
prefer forest and trees.

enlarged tip of spine   barbs

In any case, most New World porcupines climb trees and stay away from predators. The quills of a porcupine are attached loosely and pull out of its skin easily once they have stuck into something. However, porcupines cannot shoot or throw their quills. Quills are effective only when some animal comes close enough to make contact with these barbed, overdeveloped hairs.

The mammals that appear to be the best armored are the pangolins, which live in the warmer parts of Asia, Africa, and on some Pacific islands. Four kinds of pangolins are known. All are covered from head to tail with overlapping rows of flat, brown scales of keratin, each with a sharp edge.

When attacked, a pangolin rolls into a tight ball. The scales, which normally lie flat, turn with their sharp edges up, giving pangolins as much defense as a hedgehog. In addition, pangolins live in burrows, which give them added protection.

The largest pangolins grow six feet long. One smaller kind climbs trees, using its tail to wrap around branches as it goes. Sometimes pangolins walk on their hind legs and tail with their front legs held off the ground.

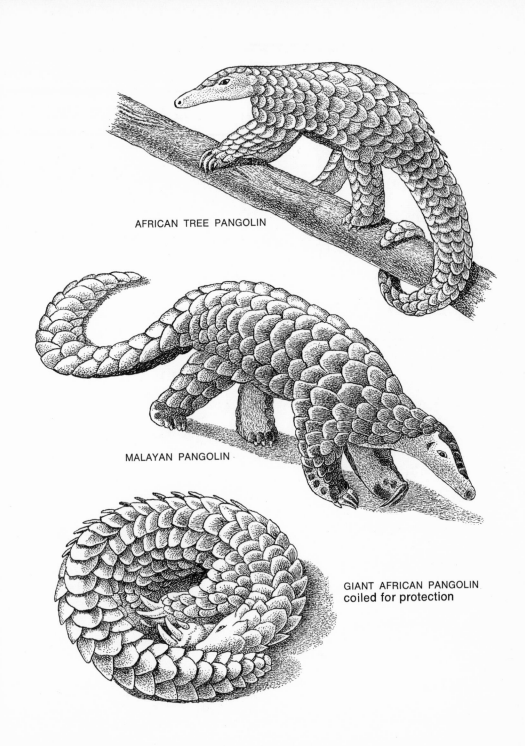

AFRICAN TREE PANGOLIN

MALAYAN PANGOLIN

GIANT AFRICAN PANGOLIN
coiled for protection

Most famous of the armored mammals are the armadillos. In fact, their name in Spanish means "little armored creatures." That description fits modern armadillos, but not the great armored armadillos that were common twenty or thirty million years ago. Some of the largest were as huge as a rhinoceros, weighed about two tons, and were much better protected.

The most armored of these ancient armadillos were the glyptodonts. The earliest fossils, some forty million years old, are of animals about a yard long. Over the years, larger and larger kinds developed. The heavily armored beasts moved slowly northward from their original home in South America and reached North America just before the Ice Age, when the climate was warmer.

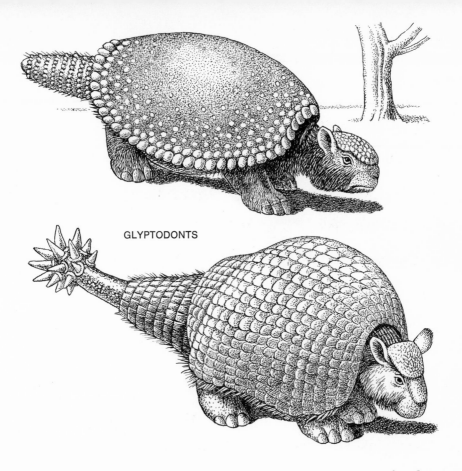

GLYPTODONTS

The largest of the glyptodonts looked something like a great turtle, twelve to fourteen feet long and equally high. Its back was made of hundreds of bony plates, usually six-sided. All the plates fitted together, forming a heavy, cup-shaped carapace.

Glyptodonts could crouch down when attacked on the open plains where they lived. Their short legs were pulled up under their carapace. They could not pull their head all the way in as a box turtle does, but bony plates on the top protected it. In defense, a glyptodont could swing its armored tail like a club. Some had rings of bone around the tail; others had tails ending in bony spikes.

Glyptodonts and other great armadillos died out about thirty thousand years ago, just as the armored dinosaurs died out many millions of years earlier. The same mystery enshrouds them both. No one is sure why glyptodonts disappeared. Did armor help or hinder their survival? Perhaps they became too heavily armored and too specialized to adapt to a changing climate and food supply.

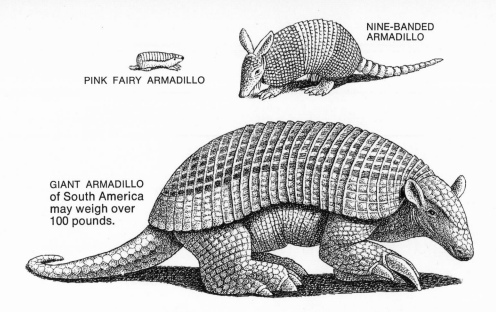

PINK FAIRY ARMADILLO

NINE-BANDED
ARMADILLO

GIANT ARMADILLO
of South America
may weigh over
100 pounds.

The smaller armadillos, still in existence today, total about twenty different kinds. They range from Argentina into the warmer parts of North America. Best known is the nine-banded armadillo, the only one living wild north of Mexico. Like most of the other species, it prefers open grassland. Often several live together in a burrow. At night they come out to feed on insects, other small animals, seeds, fruits, and bits of plants.

Armadillos have short legs with stout claws. If they cannot run from danger, they rapidly burrow into the ground or anchor themselves to the spot with their claws.

Modern armadillos are less armored than their extinct relatives. Usually there is a heavy plate over the shoulders. A similar one covers the hips. In between are a series of narrow, horny bands, each separated by flexible skin that gives armadillos some movement. Of the twenty or so species, some are named according to the number of these bands, so there are three-banded, six-banded, and nine-banded armadillos.

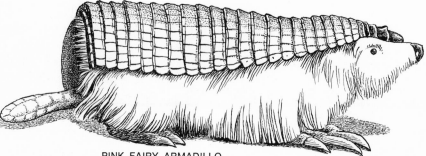

PINK FAIRY ARMADILLO

The skin between the armadillo's bands is hairy as is the skin on the underside, which lacks protection. Armadillos have hard plates on their head and sometimes on their tail. The V-shaped head and tail of the three-banded armadillo fit side by side, locking the animal into a ball when it rolls up, thus blocking entry to a predator. With both armor and burrowing habits, armadillos are well protected.

During the past century, the nine-banded armadillo has spread from Mexico far into the United States. However, cold, which it cannot stand, may keep it out of the North.

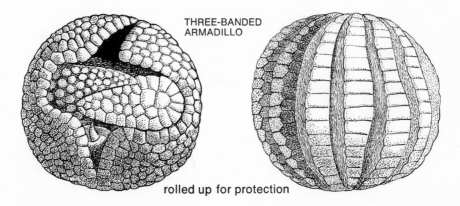

THREE-BANDED ARMADILLO

rolled up for protection

Armadillos are not the last of the armored mammals. Man himself has tried armor many times and in many places. Indians of the Pacific Northwest Coast made wooden armor. The Mayas, the ancient Japanese, Greeks, Romans, Turks, and other warrior people invented their own kinds of armor for protection in battle.

JAPANESE ARMOR
(sixteenth century)

CHAIN ARMOR
(eleventh century)

The most famous armor of all was developed in Europe some 800 years ago. Skilled craftsmen forged plates of polished steel that protected knights from head to toe. But, when he was completely armored, a knight had to be lifted with a derrick to mount his horse. Indeed, strong, heavy horses were bred to carry these heavily armored riders.

Today such armor is obsolete, yet some armor is still used by riot police and by soldiers. A crash helmet for cyclists and a hard hat for construction workers are a kind of armor—a useful form of peaceful protection against accidents.

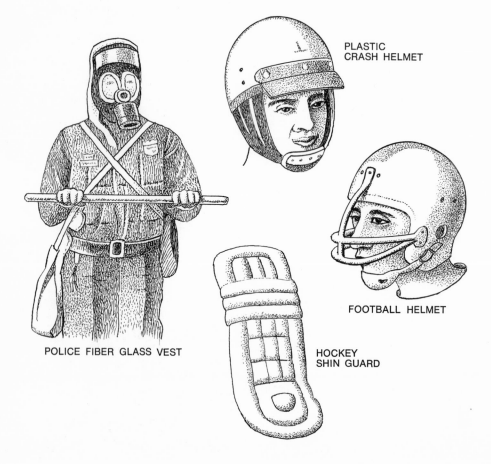

PLASTIC
CRASH HELMET

FOOTBALL HELMET

POLICE FIBER GLASS VEST

HOCKEY
SHIN GUARD

Although armored animals have survived—some for millions of years—they have not changed much to meet new conditions. Many others have changed, and they include the faster, stronger, more intelligent, and more common animals. Armor appears to isolate animals, leaving them relatively unchanged and more vulnerable as the centuries go by.

On the other hand, animals without armor live more actively and adjust to change more easily. As a result, their future seems more assured.

INDEX

Indicates illustrations